STATES

IOWA

A MyReportLinks.com Book

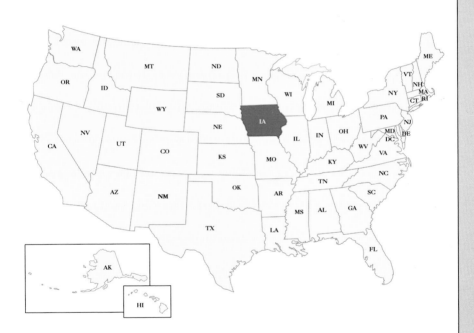

Kelly Haack

MyReportLinks.com Books

an imprint of

 Enslow Publishers, Inc.

Box 398, 40 Industrial Road

Berkeley Heights, NJ 07922

USA

MyReportLinks.com Books, an imprint of Enslow Publishers, Inc. MyReportLinks is
a trademark of Enslow Publishers, Inc.

Library of Congress Cataloging-in-Publication Data

Haack, Kelly J., 1967–
Iowa / Kelly Haack.
p. cm. — (States)
Summary: Discusses the land and climate, economy, government, and
history of the Hawkeye State. Includes Internet links to Web sites,
source documents, and photographs related to Iowa.
Includes bibliographical references (p.   ) and index.
  ISBN 0-7660-5146-3
  1. Iowa—Juvenile literature. [1. Iowa.] I. Title. II.
States (Series Berkeley Heights, N.J.)
F621.3.H33 2003
977.7—dc21
                       2003011182

Printed in the United States of America

10 9 8 7 6 5 4 3 2 1

To Our Readers:
Through the purchase of this book, you and your library gain access to the Report Links that specifically back
up this book.
The Publisher will provide access to the Report Links that back up this book and will keep these Report Links
up to date on **www.myreportlinks.com** for three years from the book's first publication date.
We have done our best to make sure all Internet addresses in this book were active and appropriate when we
went to press. However, the author and the Publisher have no control over, and assume no liability for, the
material available on those Internet sites or on other Web sites they may link to.
The usage of the MyReportLinks.com Books Web site is subject to the terms and conditions stated on the
Usage Policy Statement on **www.myreportlinks.com**.
A password may be required to access the Report Links that back up this book. The password is found on the
bottom of page 4 of this book.
Any comments or suggestions can be sent by e-mail to comments@myreportlinks.com or to the address on
the back cover.

Photo Credits: Abraham Lincoln Historical Digitization Project, p. 41; © Corel Corporation, pp. 3,
24; © 1995 PhotoDisc, pp. 13, 18, 30; © 2001 Robesus, Inc., p. 10 (flag); Department of the Interior,
p. 39; Enslow Publishers, Inc, pp. 1, 21; Franklin D. Roosevelt Presidential Library and Museum, p. 36;
Iowa Tourism Office, pp. 11, 17, 26, 44; Library of Congress, pp. 3 (Constitution), 29; Madison
County Chamber of Commerce, p. 22; MyReportLinks.com Books, p. 4; National Park Service, pp. 14,
37; Ronald Reagan Presidential Library, p. 35; The Herbert Hoover Presidential Library/Museum,
p. 43; The Iowa Legislature, p. 32.

Cover Photo: Iowa Tourism Office

Cover Description: The State Capitol, Des Moines, Iowa..

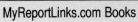
Contents

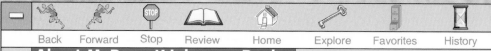

MyReportLinks.com Books
Great Books, Great Links, Great for Research!

MyReportLinks.com Books present the information you need to learn about your report subject. In addition, they show you where to go on the Internet for more information. The pre-evaluated Report Links that back up this book are kept up to date on **www.myreportlinks.com**. With the purchase of a MyReportLinks.com Books title, you and your library gain access to the Report Links that specifically back up that book. The Report Links save hours of research time and link to dozens—even hundreds—of Web sites, source documents, and photos related to your report topic.

Please see "To Our Readers" on the Copyright page for important information about this book, the MyReportLinks.com Books Web site, and the Report Links that back up this book.

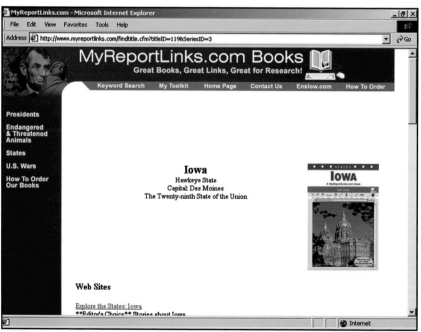

Access:

The Publisher will provide access to the Report Links that back up this book and will try to keep these Report Links up to date on our Web site for three years from the book's first publication date. Please enter **SIA8432** if asked for a password.

Report Links

 The Internet sites described below can be accessed at
http://www.myreportlinks.com

*EDITOR'S CHOICE

▶**Explore the States: Iowa**
America's Story from America's Library, a Library of Congress Web site,
tells the story of Iowa. Here you will learn what a Flying Purple Eater
is, and find stories and photos of the state of Iowa.

Link to this Internet site from http://www.myreportlinks.com

*EDITOR'S CHOICE

▶**The *World Almanac for Kids Online*: Iowa**
The *World Almanac for Kids Online* Web site features information
about Iowa's land and resources, population, education and cultural
activity, government and politics, economy, and history.

Link to this Internet site from http://www.myreportlinks.com

*EDITOR'S CHOICE

▶**Perry-Castañeda Library Map Collection: Iowa Maps**
The Perry-Castañeda Library Map Collection holds a collection of
Iowa-related maps. Here you can view maps of historical locations,
cities, and national monuments and state parks.

Link to this Internet site from http://www.myreportlinks.com

*EDITOR'S CHOICE

▶**U.S. Census Bureau: Iowa**
The U.S. Census Bureau Web site provides information about the state
of Iowa, including information related to population, business, and
geography. You will also find comparisons to statistics from previous years.

Link to this Internet site from http://www.myreportlinks.com

*EDITOR'S CHOICE

▶**The Amana Colonies**
At this National Park Service Web site you can explore the Amana
Colonies, which are located in the rolling hills of the Iowa River valley.

Link to this Internet site from http://www.myreportlinks.com

*EDITOR'S CHOICE

▶**Trail of Lewis & Clark Nebraska & Iowa**
At the Trail of Lewis & Clark Nebraska & Iowa Web site you can
take a virtual tour of the trail and learn about important findings
and attractions.

Link to this Internet site from http://www.myreportlinks.com

Report Links

The Internet sites described below can be accessed at
http://www.myreportlinks.com

▶ **The Black Hawk War of 1832**
The Black Hawk War of 1832 Web site provides a detailed overview of the
Black Hawk War, its background, and a further reading list. You will also find
a collection of maps and images.

Link to this Internet site from http://www.myreportlinks.com

▶ **Cedar Rapids Museum of Art: Grant Wood**
At the Cedar Rapids Museum of Art Web site you can read a brief description
of artist Grant Wood. You can also view many of his paintings and learn about
other exhibits at this museum.

Link to this Internet site from http://www.myreportlinks.com

▶ **Danish Immigrant Museum**
At this Web site you can take a virtual tour through the Danish Immigrant
Museum in Elkhorn, Iowa. Read about current, past, and upcoming exhibits,
the history of the museum, and Danish culture.

Link to this Internet site from http://www.myreportlinks.com

▶ **The Donna Reed Foundation for the Performing Arts**
Read the biography of film and television legend and Iowa native Donna
Reed. Learn how this foundation, which was created in her honor, encourages
talented individuals pursuing a career in the performing arts.

Link to this Internet site from http://www.myreportlinks.com

▶ **Effigy Mounds National Monument**
From the National Park Service Web site you can learn about the Effigy
Mounds, located in northeast Iowa. Click on "InDepth" to learn more about
this historic location.

Link to this Internet site from http://www.myreportlinks.com

▶ **1857 Constitution of the State of Iowa—Codified**
At this Web site you can read the full text of the Iowa State Constitution.

Link to this Internet site from http://www.myreportlinks.com

Any comments? Contact us: **comments@myreportlinks.com**

Report Links

The Internet sites described below can be accessed at
http://www.myreportlinks.com

▶ **FDR Library and Museum: Henry A. Wallace**
Read this biography of Henry A. Wallace. He was an Iowa native and
vice president of the United States under Franklin D. Roosevelt. Here
you will learn why he was considered one of the most important
figures of the New Deal.

Link to this Internet site from http://www.myreportlinks.com

▶ **Greetings from Madison County**
At the Greetings from Madison County Web site you can explore the
historic covered bridges and visit John Wayne's birthplace.

Link to this Internet site from http://www.myreportlinks.com

▶ **Herbert Clark Hoover (1929–1933)**
Herbert Hoover was the thirty-first president of the United States and
an Iowa native. At the American President Web site you will find a
comprehensive biography of his early career and presidency.

Link to this Internet site from http://www.myreportlinks.com

▶ **Infoplease.com: Iowa**
Infoplease.com provides basic facts about Iowa. Here you can view
a map of the state and the state flag. You will also learn about well-
known Iowa natives and residents.

Link to this Internet site from http://www.myreportlinks.com

▶ **Iowa Department of Natural Resources Geological Survey**
Iowa Department of Natural Resources Geological Survey Web site
features information on the mineral and water resources of the state of
Iowa. The "Browse Area" includes sections about dinosaurs, historic stone
architecture, water forms, and geodes—the state rock.

Link to this Internet site from http://www.myreportlinks.com

▶ **Iowa Official State Website**
At the Iowa Official State Web site you can learn about the governor of
Iowa. Also included is information on the government structure within
the state, facts and figures, and services offered to Iowa residents.

Link to this Internet site from http://www.myreportlinks.com

 The Internet sites described below can be accessed at
http://www.myreportlinks.com

▶**Napoléon: Politics in Napoléon's Time**
PBS's Napoléon Web site provides a comprehensive look at the French emperor. In particular, this section of the Web site discusses Napoléon's decision to sell the Louisiana territory to the United States.

Link to this Internet site from http://www.myreportlinks.com

▶**The Native Americans**
At this PBS Web site you can read about many American Indian tribes in the Iowa region, including the Oto and Sioux.

Link to this Internet site from http://www.myreportlinks.com

▶**Netstate: Iowa**
Netstate provides a basic overview of Iowa. Here you will learn about symbols, geography, people, and much more. You will also find many useful maps of Iowa at this site.

Link to this Internet site from http://www.myreportlinks.com

▶**New Perspectives on The West: William F. Cody**
PBS's New Perspectives on The West presents this history of native Iowan William F. Cody. Here you will learn about Cody and how he became known as "Buffalo Bill."

Link to this Internet site from http://www.myreportlinks.com

▶**Old Capitol Museum**
The Old Capitol Museum Web site provides a comprehensive history of the capitol building. You can also take a virtual tour of the building and view an annotated slide show of the capitol's history.

Link to this Internet site from http://www.myreportlinks.com

▶**Points of Interest of Dubuque Iowa**
The Points of Interest of Dubuque Iowa Web site explores the natural and geologic history of the Dubuque area. Here you can learn about the Mines of Spain and Crystal Lake Cave.

Link to this Internet site from http://www.myreportlinks.com

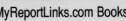
Report Links

 The Internet sites described below can be accessed at
http://www.myreportlinks.com

▶ **River of Song: Iowa: A Civic Place**
PBS's River of Song Web site contains a brief article discussing Iowa's role in American politics, and what Iowa is like culturally.

Link to this Internet site from http://www.myreportlinks.com

▶ **Senate Ratified the Louisiana Purchase Treaty October 20, 1803**
America's Story from America's Library, a Library of Congress Web site, tells the story of the Louisiana Purchase. Here you will learn how the United States acquired the land that now makes up Iowa.

Link to this Internet site from http://www.myreportlinks.com

▶ **Sioux City History**
The Sioux City History Web site offers information about notable people, historic sites, transportation, disasters, and oral histories. You will also learn about the Corn Palaces and Jolly Time popcorn!

Link to this Internet site from http://www.myreportlinks.com

▶ **State Historical Society of Iowa**
At the State Historical Society of Iowa Web site you can learn about the society's projects and historic sites. Click on "Fun Stuff" to learn state trivia.

Link to this Internet site from http://www.myreportlinks.com

▶ **Welcome to the Iowa Capitol**
At the Iowa Capitol Web site you can take a virtual tour of the capitol building in Des Moines. You will also learn about the building's history, learn facts, and view monuments on the capitol grounds.

Link to this Internet site from http://www.myreportlinks.com

▶ **The White House: Mamie Geneva Doud Eisenhower**
At the official White House Web site you can read the biography of First Lady Mamie Geneva Doud Eisenhower, who was born in Boone, Iowa.

Link to this Internet site from http://www.myreportlinks.com

▷ **Capital**
Des Moines

▷ **Population**
2,926,324*

▷ **Counties**
99

▷ **Bird**
Eastern goldfinch

▷ **Tree**
Oak

▷ **Flag**
The background is three vertical stripes—red, white, and blue. An eagle carrying blue streamers in its beak is emblazoned across the white, center stripe. The state motto is inscribed on the streamers. The word "Iowa" is written in red underneath the streamers.

▷ **Rock**
Geode

▷ **Song**
"Iowa State Song" by S. H. M. Byers

▷ **Motto**
Our Liberties We Prize, and Our Rights We Will Maintain

▷ **Gained Statehood**
December 28, 1846, the twenty-ninth state

▷ **Seal**
A citizen soldier standing in a wheat field is pictured in the center of the seal. Industrial and farming tools surround him. The Mississippi River flows in the background. Overhead, an eagle carries the state motto.

▷ **Nickname**
Hawkeye State

▷ **Flower**
Wild Rose

*Population reflects the 2000 census.

The Hawkeye State

Iowa, one of America's Midwest states, is rich in land and culture. Nestled between the Missouri and Mississippi Rivers, Iowa has some of the most fertile farmland in the world. It is also a fertile land for festivals. Around the state, people can attend an American Indian powwow, the Mexican celebration Cinco de Mayo, music and art festivals, and heritage days for Germans, Scandinavians, Italians, and other ethnic groups. With its Dutch windmills and community bands and theatres, Iowa's people thrive on homespun culture.

▲ A scene along the Mississippi River in Iowa. The Mississippi forms the state's eastern border, while the Missouri River is much of the border to the west.

In land area, Iowa ranks twenty-third in the nation. Yet it ranks top in crop production. It has only 1.6 percent of the nation's landmass but 25 percent of its grade A topsoil. One farm produces enough food to feed 279 people.[1] With 90 percent of its land used for farming, Iowa is America's breadbasket.

Because it is a farm state, Iowa's population is mostly rural. The state has more than nine hundred communities and close to 3 million people. Only two cities have more than one hundred thousand people. All of the larger cities are in Iowa's midsection from east to west.

▶ Prairie Heritage

Iowa's heritage is the land and its impact on the people who have lived there. Historically, those people were tribes of American Indian hunters and farmers. They grew corn, beans, squash, and sunflowers. They ate wild plants and hunted animals raised on the food of the rich, dark soil. Their homes were earth lodges, longhouses, and teepees, depending upon the land around them. They used their natural resources wisely. Bison provided them meat. Hides were used for clothes and shelter, and bones for tools. Pottery was made from clay earth. Their art reflected nature.

Later pioneer settlers, hungry for land, poured into Iowa. Soon the earth changed from a sea of prairie to a patchwork quilt of farms. The soil yielded its fruits to the people—corn, oats and barley, hogs, and sheep. The women raised large vegetable gardens and cared for chickens, selling eggs for profit. When crops were good, life for the settlers was good. When insects, droughts, or floods invaded the land, life was difficult.

In recent years, Iowa has diversified. Alongside growing crops and pork, Iowa is manufacturing more products

▲ *Iowa is well-known for its many cornfields. When many people think of Iowa this is what they imagine. The state, though, has much more to offer.*

and creating more service jobs. Rural communities are getting smaller. Urban communities are growing. People from different ethnic backgrounds are moving to Iowa. Recently many Hispanic Americans have decided to call Iowa home. Despite the changes, one Iowa root remains the same. The land looms large in the hearts of Iowans. In town and country, Iowa is a farm state.

▷ Iowa Attractions

The word "Iowa" causes many Americans to think of cornfields. Iowa, though, offers more than farms. In northwest Iowa, along the Minnesota border, is the Iowa Great Lakes, a vacation getaway. With its beautiful beaches, recreational opportunities, and quaint atmosphere, Okoboji, the largest Iowa Great Lakes community, attracts families. Visitors to Okoboji enjoy boating, scuba

diving, swimming, and going to Arnold's Park, a historic amusement park.

Iowa's Effigy Mounds National Monument is a peek into Iowa's past. The mounds, located along the Mississippi River in northeast Iowa, are American Indian burial sites dating as far back as 2,500 years. What makes them interesting is that they are shaped like birds and other animals.

Another peek into Iowa's past is the Amana Colonies. The colonies are a group of seven German villages that have preserved their historical roots. The original founders were settlers from Germany seeking religious freedom. In Germany they belonged to a religious group called

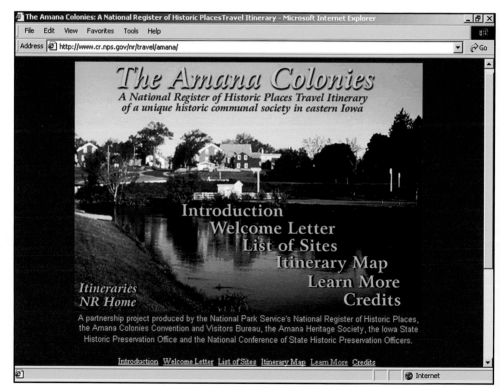

Many German immigrants settled in Iowa. The Amana Colonies is a group of seven German-American settlements.

the Community of True Inspiration. Because they were sometimes punished for their beliefs, they immigrated to the United States and settled in Iowa. In the beginning they were a communal society. Villages owned the property and buildings. Each family was given a living quarters. Each person was given a job. They worked together for the common good of the group. Today, while the Amana Colonies are no longer a communal society, the community is still important to the residents.

Other Iowa attractions are seasonal. Each summer people enter the RAGBRAI. It is a seven-day bike ride across Iowa sponsored by the *Des Moines Register*, the state's largest newspaper. The event has attracted riders from around the world. As many as twenty-three thousand bicyclists at one time have participated in RAGBRAI.[2]

In August, Iowa hosts its annual Iowa State Fair. Visitors to the fair can enjoy free entertainment such as a science show or a Wild West show. The fair attracts big-name singers such as Alicia Keys. Contests, carnival rides, and concessions are also major attractions. With about one million visitors each year, the Iowa State Fair is one of the largest fairs in the country.[3] The novel *State Fair* by Iowa author Phil Stong was based on the Iowa State Fair. The novel was later turned into a Rodgers & Hammerstein Broadway musical and three movies.

▶ Colorful Characters

Many well-known frontiersmen and media and entertainment people have come from Iowa. William "Buffalo Bill" Cody was a showman that started the famous "wild west" show that toured the United States and Europe. He learned to ride horses and do stunts in his family's pasture near Le Claire, Iowa. At age fourteen, he joined the Pony

Express, delivering mail on the longest and most dangerous stretch of the line. Later he became a soldier, United States army scout, and a buffalo hunter. It was his skill as a buffalo hunter that earned him the nickname "Buffalo Bill." Wyatt Earp was the frontier marshal who fought the legendary gunfight at the O.K. Corral in Tombstone, Arizona. He spent most of his childhood in Pella, Iowa, where he learned to shoot. Chief Black Hawk stood up for the rights of his American Indian people when the United States government forced him to move from his home in Illinois to Iowa.

Iowa is home to the nation's first creative-writing degree program and many well-known writers and artists.[4] Mark Twain, born Samuel Langhorne Clemens, sold his first piece of writing to the *Keokuk Post*. Laura Ingalls Wilder, author of the *Little House* books, spent part of her childhood near Burr Oak, Iowa. She helped her parents run the Masters Hotel. Tennessee Williams was a Pulitzer prize-winning playwright. He learned to write as a student at the University of Iowa. Tennessee Williams's real name was Thomas Lanier Williams. He got his nickname in Iowa, even though he was born in Mississippi and grew up in Missouri. The most celebrated Iowa artist is Grant Wood. He was known as the "Painter of the Soil" for painting Iowa's down-to-earth people and rolling hills. His most famous painting was *American Gothic*.

"It's a bird. It's a plane. It's Superman!" Iowa-born actor, George Reeves, was the first Superman. He was one of many Iowans to gain acclaim through entertainment. Big-screen cowboy John Wayne was born Marion Michael Morrison. He first rode a hobbyhorse in his father's drug-store in Winterset, Iowa. In 1969, John Wayne won an Academy Award for the movie *True Grit*. The Ringling

△ *This baseball field, located in Dyersville, Iowa, was the setting for the movie* Field of Dreams. *The movie is considered by many to be one of the best motion pictures about the sport.*

Brothers started their circus in Baraboo, Wisconsin, but first they lived in Iowa for many years. Comic Johnny Carson is also an Iowa native. The most famous television mom for many years was Donna Stone from the *Donna Reed Show*, played by Donna Reed. She started her life milking cows and feeding chickens on an Iowa farm.

Iowa has a rich, fertile land. With its growing diversity, it has a strong economy. In addition, Iowa has one of the best school systems in the country. The college entrance exams of Iowa students rank among the top five states. The high school graduation rate is 88 percent. That is 17 percent higher than the national average.[5]

The state is famous as the setting for the movie *Field of Dreams*. One of the characters in the movie says the line, "Is this heaven?—No, it's Iowa." Iowa is, in its own way, a "field of dreams."

Chapter 2

Land and Climate

The name "Iowa" comes from the American Indian tribe by the same name. Determining the meaning of "Iowa" is more difficult. It has been translated as "dust-in-the-faces," "drowsy ones," "he who plants pictures," and "here is the place."[1] One other translation, "beautiful land," seems to best capture Iowans' own image of their state.[2] The people of Iowa are proud of their dark rich soil, rolling hills, and shades of green, brown, and gold.

▲ Iowa's rich, dark soil allows for excellent farming. This aerial view of part of the state shows a couple of the state's many farms.

Iowa is located in the heart of the Midwest. It is bordered by six states. To the east are Illinois and Wisconsin. To the west are Nebraska and South Dakota. Minnesota is directly north of Iowa and Missouri lies directly south. Iowa is known as the "land between two rivers" because it is the only state bordered by two navigable rivers. They are the Mississippi River to the east and the Missouri River to the west.

▶ Weather Extremes

Iowa's latitude (its distance from the equator) should make the state's climate temperate, or mild. In reality, Iowa can have extremely hot, cold, and violent weather. This is because Iowa lies between the Rocky Mountains and the Appalachian Mountains. The two mountain ranges funnel cold northern and warmer southern air masses between them. These air masses collide in the Midwest, sometimes causing violent or rapidly changing weather.

Iowa has four distinct seasons. Summers are hot and humid. The temperatures average 75°F in July but have reached as hot as 118°F.[3] While the amount of snowfall in the winter is not usually large, high winds often cause long periods of bitter cold and the blowing snows that produce blizzards. In January, temperatures average 19°F but have gotten as low as −47°F.[4]

Iowa is located in central North America, which produces more tornadoes than any other area in the world. In the rainy spring, flooding can be a problem. One of the greatest natural disasters in the United States' history, the Midwest flood of 1993, devastated nine states. One of those states was Iowa. Thousands of people had to leave their homes. Fifty people in the region lost their lives. The

flooding caused $15 billion in damages. It affected all ninety-nine of Iowa's counties.[5]

Ice Age Effects

Most of Iowa is low and slopes gently. It was originally prairie land sprinkled with wildflowers. Grasses grew higher than the wheels of the wagons that crossed the prairies with pioneers. Today river bluffs, streams, and woodland mix with Iowa farmland. The northeast corner of the state stands out with its rock cliffs.

Wind, water erosion, and the glaciers of the last Ice Age have all helped to form Iowa's land. During the last Ice Age, large masses of ice called glaciers repeatedly formed and melted. The weight of the glaciers caused them to shift and move, which leveled hills, filled valleys, and brought with them rock materials called drift. Some of the drift was clay and boulders. This material is called till. Each time the land warmed up and the ice melted, flooding occurred, eroding the land and depositing more materials. Wind added to the erosion and brought with it a dirt layer called silt.[6] Silt is excellent soil for farming.

Iowa is located in a geographic region of the United States known as the Central Lowlands. Iowa can be further divided into four smaller geographic areas known as subregions. They are called the Dissected Till Plains, the Till Plains, the Western Young Drift area, and the Driftless Area.

In southern and western Iowa are the Dissected Till Plains. Glaciers were in this area only during the earlier part of the Ice Age. Later, rivers and streams flowed through the area, carrying soil and fragments of rock. As the material was swept away by water, it ground against the land and formed hills, ridges, and bluffs. This is called

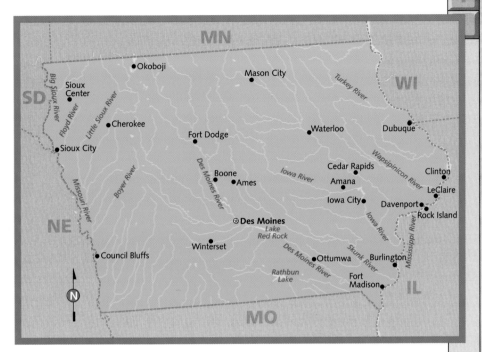

MN

Okoboji
Mason City
Sioux
Center
Turkey River
WI
SD
Big Sioux River
Floyd River
Little Sioux River
Cherokee
Fort Dodge
Waterloo
Dubuque
Sioux City
Wapsipinicon River
Cedar Rapids
Clinton
Boyer River
Missouri River
Des Moines River
Boone
Iowa River
Amana
LeClaire
Ames
Iowa City
Davenport
Rock Island
Iowa River
NE
Des Moines
Lake
Red Rock
Council Bluffs
Winterset
Des Moines River
Skunk River
Ottumwa
Burlington
Mississippi River
Rathbun
Lake
Fort
Madison
IL
N
MO

▲ *A map of Iowa.*

erosion. In the east, a narrow, flat strip of land along the Mississippi River is called the Till Plains. A few ridges formed by glaciers dot the area. Both the Till Plains and the Dissected Till Plains have rich soil called loess made from materials deposited by the glaciers.

In western Iowa, steep loess bluffs rise as high as 150 feet above the rivers. Most of northwestern Iowa is an area called the Western Young Drift section. These glacier-flattened lands are some of the best farmland in the world. Dotting the region are small lakes and swamps where glaciers left indentations in the land. The Driftless Area in northeastern Iowa is less suitable for farming. The soil deposits have blown or been washed away leaving exposed rock cliffs rising above the Mississippi River. Pine forests

cover the cliffs. This area is nicknamed "The Switzerland of America."

Watering the Land

Iowa is crisscrossed with lakes and streams. Each one flows either southeast into the Mississippi River or southwest into the Missouri River. A river that flows into another river is a tributary. The main tributaries of the Missouri River are the Big Sioux, Floyd, Little Sioux, and Boyer Rivers. The Mississippi River has longer tributaries. They include the Iowa, Des Moines, Wapsipinicon, Skunk, and Turkey Rivers. The Mississippi and Missouri

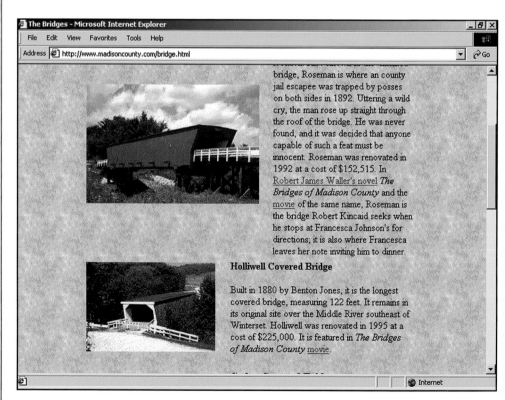

The Bridges - Microsoft Internet Explorer

File   Edit   View   Favorites   Tools   Help

Address http://www.madisoncounty.com/bridge.html

bridge, Roseman is where an county jail escapee was trapped by posses on both sides in 1892. Uttering a wild cry, the man rose up straight through the roof of the bridge. He was never found, and it was decided that anyone capable of such a feat must be innocent. Roseman was renovated in 1992 at a cost of $152,515. In Robert James Waller's novel *The Bridges of Madison County* and the movie of the same name, Roseman is the bridge Robert Kincaid seeks when he stops at Francesca Johnson's for directions; it is also where Francesca leaves her note inviting him to dinner.

Holliwell Covered Bridge

Built in 1880 by Benton Jones, it is the longest covered bridge, measuring 122 feet. It remains in its original site over the Middle River southeast of Winterset. Holliwell was renovated in 1995 at a cost of $225,000. It is featured in *The Bridges of Madison County* movie.

Internet

People come to Madison County, Iowa, to see the famous covered bridges depicted in the novel and film, The Bridges of Madison County.

rivers together stretch nearly five hundred miles and cover 200,000 acres along Iowa's border.[7] Creeks, streams and other rivers add an additional 70,000 miles of flowing water to the state.[8] About one hundred small lakes sprinkle the land. This provides a vast water supply for the residents of the state.

Rainfall and snow add more water to Iowa's plentiful supply. During an average year, Iowa receives about thirty-two inches of rain and snow. This is enough moisture for each resident to receive 11 million gallons of water per person. Most of that water soaks into the soil, watering thirsty crops.

In addition to raising crops, Iowa has several other uses for its water. Historically, the rivers helped settle the land by bringing goods and travelers into the area by ferry and barge traffic. In recent times the rivers have supplied the state with drinking, cooking, and cleaning water, recreational activities such as boating and fishing, and natural habitat for wildlife.

Iowa is habitat to a number of species of wildlife. Backyards bustle with cardinals, blue jays, squirrels, rabbits, and even an occasional white-tailed deer on the outskirts of town. Woodchuck, raccoons, badger, mink, and bobcat roam the land. Smaller animals include snakes, skunks, salamanders, and toads. Walleye, bluegill, catfish, and largemouth bass are a few of the fish that swim in the rivers and streams of the state.

Economy

From the earliest days, the natural resources of Iowa have provided its people with their livelihood. Natural resources are nature's products that are valuable to people. Early American Indians hunted large mammals such as bison and woolly mammoths. These animals provided meat to eat, skins for clothing and shelter, and bones for tools. Later groups of American Indians used clay from the earth to make pottery. They planted lush gardens of beans, squash, and corn. Corn was their most important crop. It was used to make stews and cornmeal bread, and roasted for feasts. Reed mats, willow poles, and elm bark were used to make homes.

▲ American Indians that lived in present-day Iowa hunted bison for food and clothing. Prior to European settlement, herds would graze in one area and then migrate when they used up all its natural resources.

▷ Early Trading

Archaeologists study history by digging up and examining things from the past. Archaeologists have discovered that even before Europeans came into Iowa, European goods were used in the area.[1] American Indians traveled to other parts of the country and traded furs and lead for kettles, knives, beads, guns, and other manufactured goods. Lead was easy to see in the exposed bluffs of northeast Iowa. Rivers made transporting lead an easy task. This led to extensive lead mining. Mesquaki Indians were sometimes able to earn a large income by having the men mine the lead and the women melt it down and separate it from other materials.[2]

When French, and later British and American, traders came into the region they followed the practice of American Indians and combined fur trading with lead mining. One French-Canadian businessman, Julien Dubuque, received a lead mine as a gift from the Mesquakis. He later received a large tract of land from the Spanish. This land was known as "the Lead Mines" or "Indian Diggings." Dubuque changed the name to "Mines of Spain." Today Mines of Spain is a state recreational area near Dubuque, Iowa. Starting in the mid 1800s, coal mining became an important industry to Iowa. Swedes, Italians, Croatians, and African Americans came to the state to work in the mines.[3] Since the early 1900s mining in Iowa has declined.

Steamboat and railroad transportation played an important role in Iowa's early economy. Towns sprang up first along the rivers. Railroads were considered "magic wands"[4] that promised wealth to the communities on their lines. Each of Iowa's towns developed their own

▲ *This old railway is one of many in Iowa. The railroads played a major role in the state's economy during the 1800s. If a town was located along a railway, it had a much better of prospering.*

local economy with different industries. Steamboats were manufactured at the Dubuque Boat and Boiler Company. Clinton, Iowa, had a thriving lumber industry. Buggies and carriages were manufactured in Burlington. Manufacturing and transportation remain important industries in Iowa.

▷ **Farming**

When Iowa became a territory in 1838, settlers came streaming into the state. Soon the waving sea of prairie grass gave way to the plowed fields of farmland. Iowa became an agricultural state. Today there are about ninety-seven thousand farms in Iowa.[5] In dollar amounts, Iowa ranks as the third state in the nation for farming. Only California and Texas rank higher.

Many farms in Iowa grow corn, soybeans, and oats. While these crops are mostly used to feed livestock, they can also be used for other purposes. Corn is used in making plastics and ethanol, an automobile fuel. Soybeans are turned into crayons, cleaning products, and even candles. Livestock are important to Iowa's agricultural industry. Many farmers raise cattle and pigs for beef, pork, and dairy products. The Iowa egg industry is second in the nation. It is expected to soon become first.[6] Other crops raised in Iowa include honey, grapes, strawberries, popcorn, and Christmas trees. A growing number of farmers are raising fruits and vegetables for farmers' markets and the Farmers' Market Nutrition Program. A federal program, the Farmers' Market Nutrition Program provides fruits and vegetables to women, infants, and children who are at risk for poor nutrition.[7] In addition to farming, agriculture helps the Iowa economy through manufacturing. Food processing and the production of large farm equipment are two big industries in Iowa.

Iowa farming has been changing in recent years. There are only half as many farms in the state as there were fifty years ago. Less land is being used to farm. Farmland is being used for recreation, conservation, highways, businesses, and homes. Farms are getting larger in area. Many of these changes are because of financial problems in the farm industry in the 1980s. Despite these challenges, farming remains necessary to the Iowa economy.

▷ Iowa's Changing Economy

The Iowa economy has been changing in recent years. It has been diversifying. That means that a greater variety of

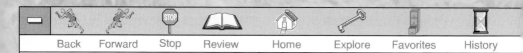
businesses have become important to Iowa's economy. More people are employed in the service industries, manufacturing, and trade than farming. The most common service industries in Iowa are business and health services. New jobs are being created in finance, insurance, real estate, and information technology. Some of the top manufacturing industries are machinery, food products, chemicals, and electronics. Government jobs, transportation, and construction also employ many people in Iowa.

Iowa has the fifth lowest unemployment rate in the nation. It has a well-educated workforce and strong academic research for new businesses. Iowa has the highest literacy rate in the nation. New job opportunities are being created. Researchers in animal and plant sciences are researching creative ways to use agricultural products.

One of Iowa's most famous researchers was George Washington Carver. In the 1890s he attended college at Simpson College in Indianola, Iowa, and Iowa State College in Ames. Carver was the first African American to graduate from Iowa State and the first to join the faculty. Later, after he moved to Alabama, Carver became famous by discovering hundreds of uses for peanuts, sweet potatoes, and other plants.

Iowa does not have any major-league sports teams, but it does have several minor-league baseball, hockey, and soccer teams. Iowa State makes its mark in college athletics as one of the schools in the Big 12 Conference. In addition, several famous athletes had Iowa connections. Dan Gable and Bruce Jenner were Olympic gold medalists. Robert "Bob" Feller, known as "Rapid Robert," jumped from high school baseball to the Cleveland Indians at age seventeen. He was elected to the National Baseball Hall of Fame in 1962.

▲ Although born in the territory that became Missouri, George Washington Carver (second from right) became the first African American to graduate from Iowa State College. He was a famous scientist and researcher.

▷ Jobs in the Arts

Dance, theatre, music, and museums are opening up jobs in the arts. History, libraries, and research are also bringing money into communities and creating new jobs. In 1987, Iowa opened a new state historical building using both private and public monies. American Indian mounds, archaeological sites, and an American Indian post are a few of the historical sites in the state that encourage tourism, bring money into communities, and help create jobs.

Chapter 4

Government

The United States purchased Iowa from France in 1803. It was a part of a larger territory called the Louisiana Purchase. Iowa did not develop any formal government until 1838 when it became an official United States territory. The first governor of the territory was John Lucas. Burlington was the first capital. Later the territorial capital was moved to Iowa City in eastern Iowa. After Iowa became a state, the capital was moved a second time. The present-day capital is Des Moines.

It took several tries for Iowa to become a state. The people did not want to pay for a state government. In

▲ The city of Des Moines is the state capital and center of government.

addition, there was some argument between the people of Iowa and the United States Congress over where the state boundaries should be. Iowa eventually became the twenty-ninth state in the union on December 26, 1846.

Structuring a Government

Before Iowa could become a state it needed to create a state government. In 1844, Iowa called a constitutional convention. A group of delegates, men appointed to represent the people of the state, convened, or met, to come up with a state constitution. A constitution is a document that describes the principles and laws by which a group of people is governed. It also tells the rights of the people. It took almost a month for the delegates to write a state constitution and two years for statehood to gain approval. In that time, a second state constitution was written. It was under the second constitution that Iowa became a state.[1]

A third constitution was written and approved in 1857. Iowa is still governed by that constitution. Since 1857, forty-six amendments, or changes, have been added to Iowa's constitution.[2] For an amendment to be added to the constitution, the state government must propose and accept the amendment. Then the people of the state must vote to approve it.

Iowa's constitution was modeled largely after the Constitution of the United States. It has a "Bill of Rights" similar to the first ten amendments of the United States Constitution. Like the U.S. government, Iowa's government has three branches.

The legislative branch makes the laws. Iowa's two-house legislature is called the general assembly. The senate has fifty members. The house of representatives has one hundred members. The people of Iowa elect the senators

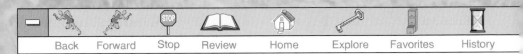

for four-year terms and the representatives for two-year terms. For bills to become laws they must be approved by both houses of the general assembly and be signed into law by the governor.

The governor is the head of the executive branch of government. In Iowa, the governor is elected to four-year terms. The governor's job is to carry out the laws of the state, lead the state military, and keep the general assembly informed about the condition of Iowa. The governor has the right to veto new laws. To veto a law means to reject it. If a bill is vetoed, two thirds of the general assembly must vote for the bill for it to become a law.

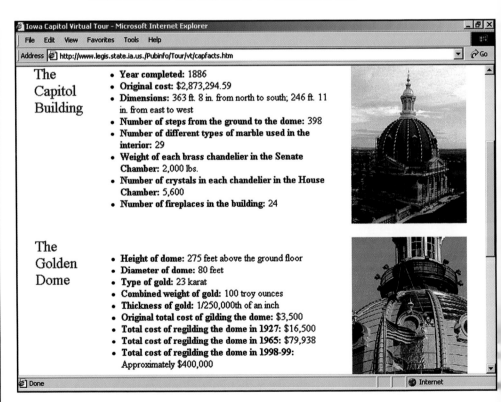

Iowa Capitol Virtual Tour – Microsoft Internet Explorer

File   Edit   View   Favorites   Tools   Help

Address | http://www.legis.state.ia.us./Pubinfo/Tour/vt/capfacts.htm | Go

The Capitol Building

- **Year completed:** 1886
- **Original cost:** $2,873,294.59
- **Dimensions:** 363 ft. 8 in. from north to south; 246 ft. 11 in. from east to west
- **Number of steps from the ground to the dome:** 398
- **Number of different types of marble used in the interior:** 29
- **Weight of each brass chandelier in the Senate Chamber:** 2,000 lbs.
- **Number of crystals in each chandelier in the House Chamber:** 5,600
- **Number of fireplaces in the building:** 24

The Golden Dome

- **Height of dome:** 275 feet above the ground floor
- **Diameter of dome:** 80 feet
- **Type of gold:** 23 karat
- **Combined weight of gold:** 100 troy ounces
- **Thickness of gold:** 1/250,000th of an inch
- **Original total cost of gilding the dome:** $3,500
- **Total cost of regilding the dome in 1927:** $16,500
- **Total cost of regilding the dome in 1965:** $79,938
- **Total cost of regilding the dome in 1998-99:** Approximately $400,000

Done   Internet

▲ The Iowa State Capitol building represents some of the finest nineteenth century architecture. The dome is made of steel and brick with a twenty-three karat gold leaf that can be seen from miles away.

The judicial branch of the government is Iowa's court system. The supreme court is the highest court. There are nine justices on Iowa's supreme court. The justices vote for the chief justice from among their members. The chief justice leads the supreme court. Under the supreme court are eight judicial districts with their own judges.

Power to the People

In Iowa, as in the United States, the people are the foundation of the government. The people have the power to elect government officials. They can voice their opinions about current local, state, and national issues. They are free to run for government and work for political change. At the national level, Iowa has two elected senators and five elected representatives in the United States Congress.

Government in Iowa starts at the local level. The state has 99 counties and 949 cities. Des Moines, with almost two hundred thousand residents, is the largest city. Delphos, with only twenty-three residents, is the state's smallest city. Iowa cities can have one of six different forms of government. The most common is the mayor-council government. In a mayor-council government the council makes the laws. The mayor manages city affairs. In Iowa, an elected board of supervisors oversees county government. Counties have several functions. Their responsibilities include law enforcement, jails, road maintenance, elections, and health codes.[3]

In the 1860s an Iowa supreme court justice, Judge John Dillon, made a ruling that would impact cities and counties throughout the United States. At the time, many local governments were corrupt. In response to the corruption, Dillon ruled that local governments had only those powers given to them by the state. All other powers

belonged to the state. Around the country, groups started pushing for an alternative form of local government known as "home rule." In states that use home rule, cities and counties have greater freedom to govern themselves. In Iowa, cities gained home rule in 1968 through the twenty-fifth amendment to the constitution. The thirty-seventh amendment in 1978 gave counties home rule.

▶ Famous Iowa Politicians

Several important politicians have come from Iowa. President Herbert Hoover and his wife Lou Henry Hoover were both natives of Iowa. Herbert Hoover was president of the United States from 1929 until 1933. Hoover was known as The Great Humanitarian. Before he became president, he led efforts to raise one billion dollars to go toward food for starving people in Belgium during World War I. During Hoover's term as president, America's economy crashed. That was the beginning of the Great Depression. President Hoover presented a federal program to feed the hungry and help farmers and businesses. It failed miserably. He also believed that much of the assistance should come from the local level, which led to him being defeated in the next election.

Ronald Reagan was the fortieth president of the United States. He was president from 1981 to 1989. Half a century before becoming president, Ronald Reagan was an Iowa sportscaster with the nickname "Dutch."[4] As president, Reagan came to be known as The Great Communicator because of his ability to grab the hearts of Americans through his speeches.

Some politicians enjoy their greatest successes outside politics. Vice President Henry A. Wallace was one such politician. Wallace was vice president from 1941 until

In 1932, after Reagan graduated from Eureka College, he went to work as a broadcaster for WOC radio station in Davenport, Iowa. He was elected the fortieth president of the United States in 1980.

1945 under Franklin D. Roosevelt. Before becoming vice president, Wallace planted his fame by raising corn. He was a corn breeder who developed hybrid corn seed. Wallace was also the secretary of agriculture from 1933 to 1940 and secretary of commerce from 1945 to 1946.

Other Government Workers

Some people with Iowa roots, while not elected politicians, had important roles in politics and government. Mamie Doud Eisenhower was born in Boone, Iowa. She was the wife of President Dwight "Ike" Eisenhower, the thirty-fourth president of the United States. Harry Hopkins was Franklin Delano Roosevelt's most trusted adviser. He even lived in the White House for awhile. Hopkins served during the Great Depression, a time when America was struggling financially. He was in charge of the New Deal, a federal program that helped impoverished Americans.

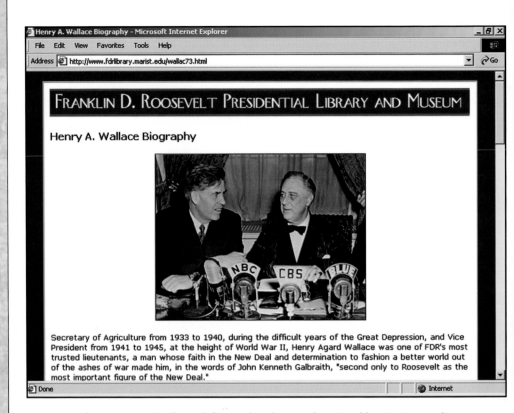

Henry A. Wallace Biography - Microsoft Internet Explorer

File Edit View Favorites Tools Help

Address http://www.fdrlibrary.marist.edu/wallac73.html

FRANKLIN D. ROOSEVELT PRESIDENTIAL LIBRARY AND MUSEUM

Henry A. Wallace Biography

Secretary of Agriculture from 1933 to 1940, during the difficult years of the Great Depression, and Vice President from 1941 to 1945, at the height of World War II, Henry Agard Wallace was one of FDR's most trusted lieutenants, a man whose faith in the New Deal and determination to fashion a better world out of the ashes of war made him, in the words of John Kenneth Galbraith, "second only to Roosevelt as the most important figure of the New Deal."

Done   Internet

▲ Henry A. Wallace (left) sits beside President Franklin D. Roosevelt during a news conference.

Arabella Mansfield was not a politician, but she was the first female lawyer in the United States. She became a lawyer in 1869. Mansfield led the Iowa women's suffrage movement to get women the right to vote in elections. Laurel Clark was born in Ames, Iowa. She worked as an astronaut for NASA. Sadly, Clark was aboard the space shuttle *Columbia* when it was lost reentering the earth's atmosphere on February 1, 2003.

History

Toward the end of the last Ice Age, nomadic Asian tribes crossed the Bering Sea from Siberia into North America. When they arrived in the land that would later become Iowa, they hunted mastodons, bison, and other large animals. As the ice receded and plants grew, they learned to gather food and plant seeds.

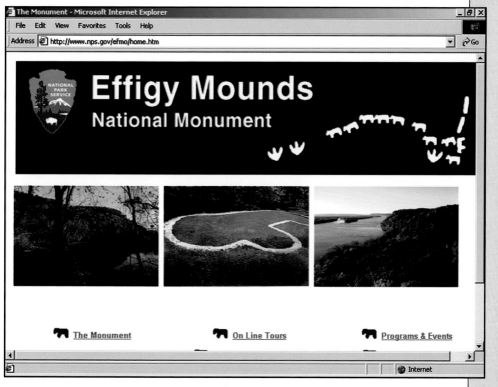

People come from all over to see the ancient American Indian burial sites at Effigy Mounds National Monument. This is the only region in North America where a culture built ceremonial mounds in the shape of animals.

Later, American Indians moved into Iowa from the Eastern Woodlands. In northeastern Iowa, some of the tribes were Mound Builders. They sculpted piles of dirt into animal shapes for burial sites. Some of their mounds can be seen at Effigy Mounds National Monument near Marquette, Iowa.

▶ A Tug-of-War for Land

French explorers Louis Joliet and Father Jacques Marquette, the first known Europeans to enter Iowa, canoed down the Mississippi River in 1673. At that time, approximately seventeen American Indian tribes lived in the state. They included the Ioway, Sauk, Mesquaki (Fox), Sioux, Potawatomi, Oto, and Missouri Indians. They fished, hunted, gathered food, and farmed. Part of the time they lived in permanent homes. Other times they followed the animal hunt.

In 1682, French explorer René-Robert Cavelier, Sieur de La Salle, claimed the entire Mississippi River and its valley for France. The territory, called Louisiana, included Iowa. La Salle's claim caused a tug-of-war for control over the region. The American Indians lived there first. Rightfully the land belonged to them. Spain and Great Britain also wanted the region.

During the French and Indian War, France secretly gave Louisiana to Spain. France hoped to keep from losing the territory to Great Britain. In 1800, Napoléon Bonaparte forced Spain to return Louisiana to France. Three years later, France sold the territory to the United States for $15 million. France needed money to fight a war in Europe. This land sale was known as the Louisiana Purchase.

President Thomas Jefferson was eager to explore Louisiana. He sent Meriwether Lewis and William Clark on an expedition up the Missouri River in 1804. The only man to die on the journey, Sergeant Charles Floyd, was buried on a river bluff near present-day Sioux City.

A year later, Zebulon Pike traveled up the Mississippi River looking for sites for forts and trading posts. The army did not listen to his suggestions and built Fort Madison in a location that upset the American Indians and was hard to defend. A few years later Commander Lieutenant Thomas Hamilton had his men secretly dig a trench from the fort to the river. The soldiers crept to their boats and canoed away. The last soldier set the fort on fire.[1]

The conflict at Fort Madison was a part of a conflict between the American Indians and the United States government known as the Indian Wars. The Indian Wars flared in Iowa and Illinois, among other areas. A treaty between the United States and the Sauk and Mesquaki

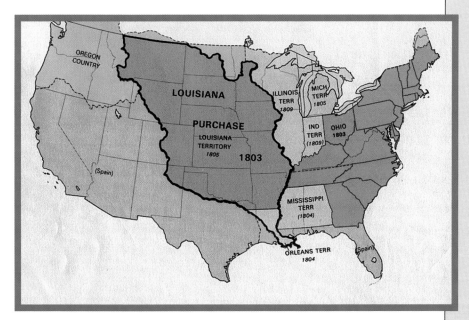

▲ In 1803, President Thomas Jefferson purchased a vast expanse of land from French emperor Napoléon. Iowa is one of the states that was carved out of that land.

Indians gave away tribal lands in Illinois. The treaty was illegal, which angered Chief Black Hawk. He and four hundred tribesmen tried to reclaim some of their land. This caused the Black Hawk War.

After the war, the Sauk and Mesquaki were forced, through the Black Hawk Purchase, to give up land in eastern Iowa. In 1857, a band of Mesquaki Indians purchased some tribal lands in Iowa back from the United States government. Their descendants live there today.

▷ Settling the State

After the Black Hawk Purchase, settlers streamed into Iowa. The first community, Dubuque, started as a lead mining community. In the late 1700s Julien Dubuque was given permission by the Mesquaki Indians and later the Spanish government to mine the area. In the 1800s Dubuque experienced a lead rush.

Most settlers sought the rich soil of the inexpensive Iowa farmland. They came from other areas in the United States and Europe looking for a better life. Settling in Iowa was difficult. Many settlers were used to woodlands, not the tall, prairie grasses of Iowa. They had to learn to build sod houses out of grass and mud, rather than wood. Families had to grow their food and make their own candles, clothing, soap, and shoes. Farmers planted corn, oats, barley, wheat, and potatoes. Plowing the land and handpicking the corn was difficult work. Most of the crops were used to feed pigs, and the pigs were then sold.

Iowa became a territory on Independence Day, July 4, 1838. The territory was about twice the size of present-day Iowa. It included parts of Minnesota, North and South Dakota, and most of present-day Iowa. At a Fort Madison celebration for the new territory, Chief Black

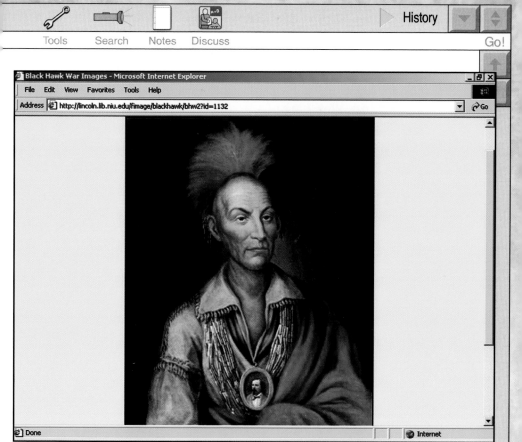

Black Hawk War Images - Microsoft Internet Explorer

File   Edit   View   Favorites   Tools   Help

Address http://lincoln.lib.niu.edu/fimage/blackhawk/bhw2?id=1132   Go

Done   Internet

▲ *In 1832, Sauk Chief, Black Hawk led the Sauk and Fox tribes out of Iowa and back to their homes in northern Illinois where they fought for their lost land.*

Hawk spoke to the group. "I shake hands with you," he told the crowd, "and as it is my wish, I hope you are my friends."[2] It took two state constitutions, a boundary dispute with Congress, and a couple votes for Iowa to become the twenty-ninth state on December 28, 1846.

▶ Fighting Battles

Iowa was a free state but some people, mostly immigrants from the South, supported slavery. Others supported the states' right to make their own decisions. The majority of Iowans supported abolition, a movement to end slavery.

Some helped slaves escape to freedom in Canada through the Underground Railroad. When the Civil War broke out between the North and South, Iowa sent seventy-five thousand men to fight with the Union.

The Civil War strengthened Iowa's commitment to the Union. People became more concerned about helping others with needs. The state joined the national economy through agriculture, technology, and the buying and selling of products. Iowa's frontier era was ending. By 1870 the population was over one million people and seven railroads crisscrossed the state.[3] Trains were powered with coal, which was mined in Iowa. Large industries popped up. Life looked positive.

However, the positive outlook did not last long. Iowa farmers began to struggle financially. When southern farms began producing again, crop prices fell. Costs were high and farmers went into debt. Locust swarms destroyed fields. The state also struggled with social issues. People argued over voting rights. Iowa became the first state to give African Americans the right to vote. It took women more than fifty years to gain that right. Iowans approved an amendment making alcohol illegal. The movement to make alcohol illegal was called Prohibition.

▶ A Positive Present

Modern Iowa emerged strong. Immigrants from Germany and Scandinavia brought with them religious diversity and a priority for education and literacy.[4] At the end of the 1800s Iowa entered the "Golden Age of Agriculture." Technology and high crop prices helped the farmers become prosperous. Industries grew. Several cities opened meatpacking plants. Quaker Oats opened in Cedar Rapids. John Deere tractors were manufactured in

Born on August 10, 1874 in West Branch, Iowa, Herbert Hoover was the thirty-first president of the United States. Unfortunately, Hoover was blamed by some for the Great Depression that gripped the country in the late 1920s and 1930s.

Waterloo. The Maytag Company in Newton, Iowa, became known for making electric washing machines.

About the same time, Iowans started to work to reform, or change, some of the problems facing the state. Railroad laws helped farmers ship their products for fair prices. New laws ensured that workers were paid fairly, had safe working conditions, received financial help when they were hurt on the job, and were not forced to work long hours. Women were given the right to vote in local elections. Safe food and public health and safety laws were passed. Education was strengthened. Parks and roads were built. This was known as the Progressive Era.

Many Iowans were of German heritage. During World War I, those Iowans suffered because of the anti-German feelings in the country. The Germans had been the enemy, and German Americans were looked upon with suspicion. After World War I, Iowa again had economic troubles, along with the rest of the nation. Yet the state remained strong in arts, education, and culture. After World War II, the economy turned around. Industry

▲ The Iowa State Fair is an event where all Iowans can enjoy one another's company, and what the state has to offer. Iowa is on the rise, both economically and culturally.

boomed. Military equipment was manufactured. Farm products were needed for the war.

Iowa has remained prosperous. The only slump was during the farm crisis of the 1980s when farm prices and land value fell. This led to a more balanced economy. In 1991, legalized riverboat gambling began in Iowa. This was controversial. Some people felt it would strengthen the economy. Others were concerned gambling would create social problems.[5]

The citizens of Iowa continue to debate political and social issues. The arts continue to grow. As more minorities move into Iowa, the state is being enriched culturally. Iowa looks forward to a bright future.

Chapter 1. The State of Iowa

1. Diane Landau, *Iowa: The Spirit of America* (New York: Harry N. Abrams, Inc., 1998), p. 48.

2. Dave Harrenstein, "30th Anniversary RAGBRAI XXX 2002," *RAGBRAI Web Site*, n.d., <http://www.ragbrai.org/factoids.htm> (June 15, 2002).

3. Marketing Department, "Milestone Moment in 148-Year History: 1,008,000 Visitors Make 'The Big One' Biggest Ever," *Iowa State Fair*, n.d., <http://www.iowastatefair.org/thefair.html> (October 25, 2002).

4. Winston Barclay, "UI Writers: The Workshop," *The Writer's Workshop*, 1997,<http://www.uiowa.edu/~iww/iww2.htm> (October 25, 2002).

5. Secretary of State, "Iowa Profile: Quick Facts About Iowa," *Iowa Official Register 1999–2000*, n.d., <http://www.sos.state.ia.us/publications/redbook/profile/8-14.html> (June 15, 2002).

Chapter 2. Land and Climate

1. Carl A. Merry, "The Historic Period," *Office of the State Archaeologist, University of Iowa*, 1996, <http://www.uiowa.edu/~osa/learn/historic/hisper.htm> (October 28, 2002).

2. Ibid.

3. Dorothy Schwieder, "State of Iowa History," Iowa-Counties.com, *Kade LLC*, n.d., <http://www.iowa-counties.com/historical/iowahistory.htm> (October 28, 2002).

4. Dorothy Schwieder, *Iowa: The Middle Land* (Ames: Iowa State University Press, 1996), p. 59.

5. Secretary of State, "Agriculture—Iowa's Basic Industry," *Iowa Official Register 1999–2000*, n.d., <http:www.sos.state.ia.us/publications/redbook/profile/8-7.html> (October 28, 2002).

6. Ibid.

7. Ibid.

8. Iowa Department of Natural resources, *Iowa—Portrait of the Land* (Des Moines: State of Iowa, 2000), p. 58.

Chapter 3. Economy

1. Dorothy Schwieder, Thomas Morain, and Lynn Nielsen, *Past to Present: The People and the Prairie*, 2nd Edition (Ames: Iowa State University Press, 1991), pp. 16–20.

2. Carl A. Merry, "The Historic Period," *Office of the State Archeologist, University of Iowa,* 1996, <http://www.uiowa.edu/~osa/learn/historic/hisper.htm> (October 28, 2002).

3. Schwieder, Morain, and Nielsen, pp. 20–21.

4. Merry, "The Historic Period."

5. Ibid.

6. Dorothy Schwieder, *Iowa: The Middle Land.* (Ames: Iowa State University Press, 1996), p. 59.

7. Ibid. pp. 57–58.

Chapter 4. Government

1. Steven C. Cross, "The Drafting of Iowa's Constitution," *Iowa Official Register 1999–2000,* n.d., <http:www.sos.state.ia.us/publications/redbook/history/7-6.html> (October 31, 2002).

2. Secretary of State, "Amendments to the Constitution of Iowa," *Iowa Official Register 1999–2000,* n.d., <http:www.sos.state.ia.us/publications/redbook/history/7-8.html> (October 31, 2002).

3. Secretary of State, "County Government," *Iowa Official Register 1999–2000,* n.d., <http:www.sos.state.ia.us/publications/redbook/local/6-1.html> (October 31, 2002).

4. Tom Longden, "Famous Iowans—Ronald Reagan," *Des Moines Register,* n.d., <http://www.desmoinesregister.com/extras/iowans/reagan.html> (October 31, 2002).

Chapter 5. History

1. Dorothy Schwieder, *Iowa: The Middle Land,* (Ames: Iowa State University Press, 1996), pp. 21–22.

2. Ibid., p. 28.

3. Margaret Atherton Bonney, "Prairie Voices Iowa Heritage Collection: A Brief Overview of Iowa History," *State Historical Society of Iowa,* n.d., <http://www.iowahistory.org/education/heritage_curriculum/iowahistory_overview.htm> (November 1, 2002).

4. Ibid.

5. Schwieder, pp. 320–321.

Further Reading

Aylesworth, Thomas G. and Virginia L. *Western Great Lakes: Illinois, Iowa, Minnesota, Wisconsin.* Broomall, Pa.: Chelsea House Publishers, 1995.

Balcavage, Dynise. *Iowa—From Sea to Shining Sea.* Danbury, Conn.: Children's Press, 2002.

Fradin, Dennis Brindell. *Iowa.* Danbury, Conn.: Children's Press, 1995.

Hintz, Martin. *Iowa—America the Beautiful, Second Series.* Danbury, Conn.: Children's Press, 2000.

Kavanagh, James. *Iowa Birds.* Blaine, Wash.: Waterford Press, 1999.

Kummer, Patricia K. *Iowa.* Minnetonka, Minn.: Capstone Press, Inc., 2003.

Martin, Michael E. and Michael A. Martin. *Iowa: The Hawkeye State—World Almanac Library of the States.* Milwaukee, Wis.: World Almanac Education Group, 2002.

Morrice, Polly. *Iowa—Celebrate the States.* Tarrytown, New York: Benchmark Books, 1998.

Runkel, Sylvan T. and Dean M. Roosa. *Wildflowers and Other Plants of Iowa Wetlands.* Ames, Iowa: Iowa State University Press, 1999.

Thompson, Kathleen. *Iowa—Portrait of America.* Austin, Tex.: Raintree Steck-Vaughn, 1996.

Index